Get Rich

How to Build Long-Term Wealth Through Property Investment

NELLA BYRAN

Copyright

No part of this should be reproduced without the permission of the author.

© **Nella Byran 2024**

Contents

Opening 6
Foundations of Fortune 9
Insider Insights 14
Unveiling Hidden Gems 18
Crafting Your Investment Plan 22
Financial Mastery: Navigating Property Financing ... 27
Market Mastery: Trends and Tactics for Growth 32
Shielding Your Assets 37
Closing Deals with Confidence 42
Renovation Strategies 47
Maximizing Income through Leasing 52
Strategic Expansion 57
Global Ventures: Exploring International Real Estate 62
Strength in Numbers: The Power of Real Estate Partnerships 68
Retire Rich: Real Estate as Your Key to Financial Freedom 73
Learning from Mistakes: Avoiding Common Pitfalls 78
Innovation in Action 83
Generational Wealth with Real Estate 88
Closing 93

Opening

Welcome to the world of wealth creation through property investment – where fortunes are forged, dreams are realized, and legacies are built. In "Get Rich: How to Build Long-Term Wealth Through Property Investment," we embark on an exhilarating journey through the dynamic landscape of real estate, uncovering the strategies, insights, and secrets that pave the way to prosperity.

In these pages, you'll discover the foundational principles that underpin the creation of wealth in real estate. From understanding the intricate dynamics of market trends to mastering the art of negotiation, each chapter is meticulously crafted to equip you with the knowledge and skills necessary to thrive in this competitive arena.

We delve deep into the core strategies that drive property investment success, offering insider insights gleaned from years of experience and expertise. Whether you're a seasoned investor looking to expand your portfolio or a novice eager to take your first steps, "Get Rich" provides a comprehensive roadmap to guide you towards your financial goals.

But success in real estate isn't just about knowing where to buy – it's also about when to buy and how to maximize the potential of every investment opportunity. From selecting prime locations to implementing renovation strategies that add value, we leave no stone unturned in our quest to uncover the hidden gems that lie within the property market.

Moreover, we explore the crucial role of financial mastery in navigating the complexities of property financing, as well as the importance of effective risk management in safeguarding your assets. Through real-life case studies and practical examples, you'll learn how to leverage market trends and tactics to your advantage, ensuring sustainable growth and long-term prosperity.

"Get Rich" isn't just a book – it's a blueprint for building a lasting legacy of wealth and financial freedom. Whether your goal is to retire comfortably, leave a legacy for future generations, or simply enjoy the fruits of your labor, the principles and strategies outlined within these pages will empower you to turn your dreams into reality.

So, join us as we embark on this transformative journey through the world of real estate investment. Let "Get Rich" be your guide as you unlock the doors to unlimited potential and embark on a path towards a future filled with prosperity, abundance, and lasting success.

Foundations of Fortune

"Foundations of Fortune: Building Wealth in Real Estate" serves as the cornerstone upon which every successful property investor builds their empire. In this chapter, we delve deep into the fundamental principles and strategies that lay the groundwork for long-term wealth creation in the dynamic world of real estate.

At the heart of building wealth in real estate lies the concept of strategic property acquisition. This involves identifying and investing in properties with the potential for significant appreciation over time. Whether it's through capitalizing on emerging market trends, selecting properties in high-demand locations, or targeting undervalued assets ripe for growth, strategic acquisition forms the bedrock of a successful investment portfolio.

Understanding the intricacies of market cycles is essential for investors seeking to build wealth in real estate. Markets fluctuate, and being able to identify and capitalize on opportunities during various stages of the cycle is key to maximizing returns. From boom periods characterized by rapid price appreciation to downturns offering lucrative buying opportunities, adept investors navigate these cycles with foresight and agility, positioning themselves for long-term success.

In addition to strategic acquisition and market timing, effective property management plays a crucial role in building wealth in real estate. Maximizing the income potential of rental properties through efficient management practices, tenant selection, and proactive maintenance not only ensures consistent cash flow but also enhances property value over time. Furthermore, leveraging technology and automation can streamline management processes, freeing up time and resources to focus on expanding the investment portfolio.

Diversification is a cornerstone of any robust investment strategy, and real estate is no exception. By diversifying across different property types, locations, and investment strategies, investors can mitigate risk and optimize returns. Whether it's residential, commercial, industrial, or mixed-use properties, each asset class offers unique opportunities for wealth creation, and a well-diversified portfolio ensures resilience against market fluctuations and economic downturns.

Financing strategies play a pivotal role in building wealth in real estate. Leveraging other people's money (OPM) through mortgages, private loans, or creative financing techniques allows investors to amplify their purchasing power and acquire properties with minimal out-of-pocket expenses. However, prudent financial management is essential to avoid overleveraging and ensure sustainable growth.

Cultivating a long-term mindset is paramount for investors seeking to build wealth in real estate. While short-term gains may be enticing, it's the patient accumulation of assets and the compounding effect of appreciation, rental income, and tax benefits that truly drive wealth creation over time. By adopting a disciplined approach, staying abreast of market trends, and continually seeking opportunities for growth, investors can lay a solid foundation for building lasting wealth in real estate.

Finally, "Foundations of Fortune: Building Wealth in Real Estate" encapsulates the essential principles and strategies that underpin success in the world of property investment. By mastering the art of strategic acquisition, navigating market cycles, implementing effective management practices, diversifying portfolios, leveraging financing strategies, and maintaining a long-term perspective, investors can forge a path towards financial freedom and prosperity in the dynamic realm of real estate.

Insider Insights

"Insider Insights: Strategies for Property Investment Success" unlocks the door to the inner workings of the real estate investment world, providing invaluable knowledge and tactics gleaned from seasoned experts and industry insiders. In this chapter, we delve deep into the strategies that separate successful investors from the rest, offering a comprehensive roadmap to navigate the complexities of property investment with confidence and finesse.

First and foremost, successful property investment begins with thorough research and due diligence. By conducting comprehensive market analysis, investors can identify emerging trends, evaluate supply and demand dynamics, and pinpoint areas poised for growth. Whether it's analyzing demographic trends, economic indicators, or zoning regulations, the ability to gather and interpret data is critical for making informed investment decisions.

Successful investors understand the importance of aligning their investment strategy with their financial goals and risk tolerance. Whether you're a conservative investor seeking stable, long-term returns or a more aggressive investor pursuing higher-risk, higher-reward opportunities, tailoring your strategy to align with your objectives is essential for achieving success in the competitive real estate market.

Successful investors possess a keen eye for value and opportunity. Whether it's identifying distressed properties ripe for renovation, negotiating favorable purchase terms, or spotting undervalued assets in high-demand locations, the ability to recognize hidden gems and capitalize on them is a hallmark of successful property investors.

In addition, successful investors leverage their networks and relationships to uncover opportunities and gain access to valuable resources. Whether it's collaborating with real estate agents, networking with fellow investors, or partnering with industry professionals, building a strong support system can provide invaluable insights, advice, and opportunities that can propel your investment journey forward.

However, successful investors are proactive in managing their portfolios, continually seeking ways to optimize performance and maximize returns. Whether it's implementing cost-saving measures, optimizing rental rates, or reinvesting profits into additional properties, proactive portfolio management is essential for staying ahead of the curve and adapting to changing market conditions.

Also, successful investors understand the importance of continuous learning and self-improvement. Whether it's staying abreast of industry trends, attending workshops and seminars, or seeking mentorship from experienced investors, the pursuit of knowledge and expertise is a lifelong journey that fuels success in the ever-evolving world of real estate investment.

In conclusion, "Insider Insights: Strategies for Property Investment Success" provides a roadmap to success in the competitive world of real estate investment. By conducting thorough research, aligning investment strategies with financial goals, recognizing value and opportunity, leveraging networks and relationships, proactive portfolio management, and continuous learning, investors can unlock the secrets to building wealth and achieving success in the dynamic realm of property investment.

Unveiling Hidden Gems

"Unveiling Hidden Gems: Mastering Location Selection" is a crucial chapter that delves into one of the most pivotal aspects of successful property investment: choosing the right location. In the intricate tapestry of real estate, location isn't just a factor; it's the foundation upon which the entire investment rests. This chapter uncovers the strategies and insights necessary to identify and capitalize on hidden gems—those overlooked or undervalued locations with the potential for significant appreciation and long-term growth.

First and foremost, mastering location selection begins with understanding the key drivers of value in real estate. Factors such as proximity to amenities, schools, transportation hubs, and employment centers can significantly influence property demand and appreciation potential. By analyzing demographic trends, economic indicators, and infrastructure developments, investors can identify areas primed for growth and investment.

Successful investors recognize the importance of conducting thorough due diligence when evaluating potential locations. This involves researching local market conditions, vacancy rates, rental yields, and historical property performance to assess the investment viability of a particular area. By leveraging data-driven analysis and market research tools, investors can make informed decisions and mitigate the risks associated with location selection.

Mastering location selection requires a keen understanding of market dynamics and emerging trends. While established neighborhoods may offer stability and liquidity, emerging or transitional areas often present unique opportunities for growth and value appreciation. By identifying early indicators of gentrification, revitalization, or infrastructure development, investors can position themselves ahead of the curve and capitalize on the potential upside of up-and-coming neighborhoods.

In addition, successful investors employ a multifaceted approach to location selection, considering both macro and micro factors that influence property value and investment performance. While macroeconomic trends and city-wide developments provide a broader context for investment decisions, micro-level factors such as neighborhood demographics, crime rates, and school districts can significantly impact property demand and desirability.

Mastering location selection involves thinking beyond the present and anticipating future trends and developments. Whether it's identifying emerging lifestyle preferences, demographic shifts, or technological advancements, forward-thinking investors position themselves to capitalize on evolving market dynamics and consumer preferences. By staying ahead of the curve and adapting to changing market conditions, investors can maximize their investment returns and build a resilient portfolio over time.

In essence "Unveiling Hidden Gems: Mastering Location Selection" is a critical chapter that equips investors with the knowledge and strategies necessary to identify and capitalize on hidden gems in the real estate market. By understanding the key drivers of value, conducting thorough due diligence, recognizing emerging trends, and adopting a forward-thinking approach, investors can master the art of location selection and unlock the potential for long-term wealth creation in the dynamic world of property investment.

Crafting Your Investment Plan

"Blueprint for Prosperity: Crafting Your Investment Plan" serves as the architectural design for your journey towards wealth creation in real estate. In this pivotal chapter, we delve into the essential elements of crafting a strategic investment plan tailored to your financial goals, risk tolerance, and investment objectives. Just as a blueprint guides the construction of a building, your investment plan provides the framework for building a successful and sustainable real estate portfolio.

The first step in crafting your investment plan is defining your financial goals and objectives. Whether your aim is to generate passive income, achieve capital appreciation, build a retirement nest egg, or leave a legacy for future generations, clarifying your objectives provides the guiding light for your investment journey. By setting specific, measurable, achievable, relevant, and time-bound (SMART) goals, you create a roadmap that aligns your actions with your aspirations.

Crafting your investment plan involves conducting a comprehensive assessment of your risk tolerance and investment horizon. Real estate investing encompasses a spectrum of risk profiles, from conservative income-generating properties to high-risk, high-reward development projects. By understanding your risk tolerance and time horizon, you can tailor your investment strategy to align with your comfort level and long-term objectives.

Your investment plan should outline the asset allocation strategy that will guide your portfolio construction. This involves determining the optimal mix of asset classes, such as residential, commercial, industrial, and mixed-use properties, as well as considering alternative investments like real estate investment trusts (REITs), private equity funds, or crowdfunding platforms. By diversifying across different asset classes, you can mitigate risk and optimize returns in varying market conditions.

In addition, crafting your investment plan entails conducting thorough market research and due diligence to identify investment opportunities that align with your objectives. This involves analyzing market trends, evaluating supply and demand dynamics, and assessing the potential risks and rewards of specific investment opportunities. By leveraging data-driven analysis and market research tools, you can make informed investment decisions and maximize the potential for success.

Investment plan should outline the financing strategy that will fund your real estate acquisitions. Whether you opt for traditional bank financing, private loans, seller financing, or creative financing techniques, securing the necessary capital is essential for executing your investment plan. By evaluating financing options based on factors such as interest rates, terms, and leverage ratios, you can optimize your capital structure and maximize returns on investment.

Crafting your investment plan involves establishing clear criteria for property selection and acquisition. This includes defining the target market, property type, location preferences, and investment criteria that align with your overall strategy. By creating a screening process and investment checklist, you can streamline the decision-making process and focus your efforts on properties that meet your investment criteria.

In conclusion, "Blueprint for Prosperity: Crafting Your Investment Plan" lays the foundation for building a successful and sustainable real estate portfolio. By defining your financial goals, assessing your risk tolerance, determining asset allocation, conducting market research, securing financing, and establishing criteria for property selection, you create a roadmap that guides your investment journey towards prosperity and wealth creation in the dynamic world of real estate.

Financial Mastery: Navigating Property Financing

"Financial Mastery: Navigating Property Financing" is a critical chapter in the journey of real estate investment, where understanding the intricacies of property financing is key to unlocking opportunities and maximizing returns. In this chapter, we delve deep into the strategies and techniques that empower investors to navigate the complex landscape of property financing with confidence and mastery.

At the heart of financial mastery in real estate is understanding the various financing options available to investors. From traditional mortgages and bank loans to private financing, seller financing, and creative financing techniques, each option presents unique advantages and considerations. By evaluating the terms, interest rates, repayment schedules, and associated costs of each financing option, investors can select the most suitable option that aligns with their investment strategy and financial objectives.

Navigating property financing requires a thorough understanding of the factors that influence loan approval and terms. Lenders assess various factors such as creditworthiness, income stability, debt-to-income ratio, and property valuation when evaluating loan applications. By proactively managing credit, maintaining financial stability, and presenting a strong loan application package, investors can enhance their chances of securing favorable financing terms and maximizing leverage.

Successful property financing involves optimizing the capital structure to maximize returns and mitigate risk. This may involve leveraging other people's money (OPM) to amplify purchasing power and acquire properties with minimal out-of-pocket expenses. However, prudent financial management is essential to avoid overleveraging and ensure sustainable growth. By striking the right balance between debt and equity, investors can optimize their capital structure and enhance overall investment returns.

In addition, navigating property financing requires proactive management of cash flow and financial resources. This involves developing robust financial projections, budgeting for operating expenses, and maintaining adequate reserves to cover unexpected expenses or vacancies. By implementing sound financial management practices and monitoring cash flow closely, investors can ensure the long-term viability and profitability of their real estate investments.

Successful investors leverage financing strategies to enhance investment returns and optimize tax efficiency. This may include utilizing tax-advantaged financing structures, such as 1031 exchanges, opportunity zone investments, or utilizing depreciation deductions to offset rental income. By understanding the tax implications of different financing options and structuring investments accordingly, investors can minimize tax liabilities and maximize after-tax returns on investment.

Furthermore, navigating property financing involves staying abreast of market trends and regulatory changes that may impact financing availability and terms. Changes in interest rates, lending policies, or economic conditions can affect the cost and availability of financing, necessitating adaptability and foresight in financial decision-making. By staying informed and agile, investors can position themselves to capitalize on opportunities and navigate challenges in the dynamic real estate market.

In conclusion, "Financial Mastery: Navigating Property Financing" is a critical component of real estate investment success, empowering investors to leverage financing options effectively and optimize investment returns. By understanding financing options, optimizing capital structure, managing cash flow, maximizing tax efficiency, and staying informed of market trends, investors can navigate the complex landscape of property financing with confidence and mastery, unlocking the full potential of their real estate investments.

Market Mastery: Trends and Tactics for Growth

"Market Mastery: Trends and Tactics for Growth" is an indispensable chapter that unveils the strategies and insights necessary to navigate the ever-evolving landscape of the real estate market. In this dynamic realm, success hinges on the ability to anticipate trends, capitalize on opportunities, and adapt to changing market conditions with agility and foresight. This chapter serves as a compass, guiding investors through the intricacies of market dynamics and equipping them with the tools and tactics needed to achieve sustainable growth and success.

First and foremost, mastering the real estate market requires a deep understanding of prevailing trends and macroeconomic forces shaping the industry. Whether it's demographic shifts, urbanization patterns, technological advancements, or regulatory changes, staying abreast of market trends enables investors to identify emerging opportunities and adjust their investment strategies accordingly. By analyzing market data, economic indicators, and industry reports, investors can gain valuable insights into market dynamics and position themselves ahead of the curve.

Successful investors leverage tactical approaches to capitalize on market opportunities and optimize investment returns. This may involve identifying niche markets or subsectors with strong growth potential, such as multifamily housing, student housing, senior living, or emerging tech hubs. By focusing on specialized segments of the market, investors can mitigate competition and enhance their ability to generate outsized returns.

Market mastery entails employing strategic marketing and positioning strategies to attract tenants, buyers, or investors. This may include leveraging digital marketing channels, staging properties for maximum appeal, or highlighting unique selling points to differentiate properties from the competition. By understanding the preferences and needs of target demographics, investors can enhance property desirability and maximize occupancy rates or sales prices.

In addition, mastering the real estate market involves adopting innovative technologies and tools to streamline operations and enhance decision-making. Whether it's using data analytics to identify investment opportunities, virtual reality to showcase properties remotely, or blockchain technology to streamline transactions, embracing innovation enables investors to gain a competitive edge and unlock new avenues for growth and efficiency.

Moreover, successful investors diversify their portfolios and employ risk management strategies to safeguard against market volatility and mitigate downside risk. This may involve diversifying across different asset classes, geographic regions, or investment strategies to spread risk and optimize returns. Additionally, employing hedging strategies, such as options or futures contracts, can provide protection against adverse market movements and preserve capital in uncertain times.

Also, market mastery requires maintaining a long-term perspective and resisting the temptation to succumb to short-term market fluctuations or fads. By focusing on fundamental investment principles, such as cash flow, value appreciation, and risk management, investors can weather market cycles and achieve sustainable growth over time. Additionally, employing disciplined investment criteria and adhering to predefined investment strategies enables investors to avoid impulsive decisions and stay on course towards their long-term objectives.

In conclusion, "Market Mastery: Trends and Tactics for Growth" equips investors with the knowledge, strategies, and tools needed to navigate the complexities of the real estate market successfully. By understanding market trends, employing tactical approaches, leveraging technology, diversifying portfolios, and maintaining a long-term perspective, investors can achieve sustainable growth and success in the dynamic world of real estate investment.

Shielding Your Assets

"Shielding Your Assets: Effective Risk Management" is a pivotal chapter that underscores the importance of safeguarding your investments in the unpredictable landscape of real estate. In this chapter, we explore the strategies and techniques necessary to identify, assess, and mitigate risks, ensuring the preservation of wealth and the longevity of your investment portfolio.

First and foremost, effective risk management begins with a comprehensive understanding of the various risks inherent in real estate investment. These may include market risk, such as fluctuations in property values or rental demand; financial risk, such as interest rate fluctuations or liquidity constraints; operational risk, such as maintenance issues or tenant turnover; and regulatory risk, such as zoning changes or environmental regulations. By identifying and categorizing potential risks, investors can develop proactive strategies to mitigate their impact.

Successful investors employ a diversified approach to risk management, spreading their investments across different asset classes, geographic locations, and investment strategies. By diversifying their portfolios, investors can reduce exposure to any single risk factor and enhance overall portfolio resilience. Additionally, diversification allows investors to capture opportunities in different market segments and mitigate the impact of adverse market movements on their overall investment performance.

Effective risk management entails conducting thorough due diligence when evaluating investment opportunities. This involves researching market conditions, conducting property inspections, reviewing financial statements, and assessing potential liabilities to identify any red flags or potential risks. By performing rigorous due diligence, investors can avoid costly mistakes and make informed decisions that align with their risk tolerance and investment objectives.

In addition, successful investors leverage insurance and risk mitigation tools to protect their investments against unforeseen events and liabilities. This may include property insurance to cover damages or losses, liability insurance to protect against lawsuits or claims, and title insurance to safeguard against title defects or ownership disputes. Additionally, investors may use risk management techniques such as option contracts, derivatives, or hedging strategies to mitigate financial risks and protect against adverse market movements.

Effective risk management involves implementing proactive measures to mitigate operational risks and enhance property resilience. This may include implementing preventive maintenance programs to address potential issues before they escalate, conducting regular property inspections to identify maintenance needs, and implementing robust tenant screening processes to minimize the risk of default or delinquency. Additionally, maintaining adequate reserves and contingency funds can provide a buffer against unexpected expenses or income disruptions.

Furthermore, successful investors stay informed and adaptable, continually monitoring market conditions and adjusting their strategies in response to changing circumstances. By staying abreast of industry trends, regulatory changes, and economic indicators, investors can anticipate potential risks and opportunities and adjust their investment approach accordingly. Additionally, maintaining open communication with tenants, property managers, and other stakeholders can provide valuable insights into emerging risks and enable proactive risk mitigation strategies.

In conclusion, "Shielding Your Assets: Effective Risk Management" is a critical component of real estate investment success, ensuring the preservation of wealth and the longevity of your investment portfolio. By understanding the various risks inherent in real estate investment, diversifying portfolios, conducting thorough due diligence, leveraging insurance and risk mitigation tools, implementing proactive measures, and staying informed and adaptable, investors can shield their assets against potential threats and achieve sustainable growth and success in the dynamic world of real estate investment.

Closing Deals with Confidence

"Mastering Negotiation: Closing Deals with Confidence" is a pivotal chapter that delves into the art and science of negotiation in the realm of real estate investment. In this chapter, we explore the strategies, tactics, and mindset necessary to navigate the negotiation process with confidence and finesse, ensuring favorable outcomes and maximizing investment returns.

Negotiation lies at the heart of every successful real estate transaction, whether it's securing favorable purchase terms, negotiating rental agreements, or structuring financing arrangements. At its core, negotiation is a collaborative process of communication and compromise, where parties seek to reconcile their interests and reach mutually beneficial agreements. Mastering negotiation empowers investors to assertively advocate for their interests, overcome obstacles, and close deals with confidence.

First and foremost, successful negotiators approach the negotiation process with a clear understanding of their objectives and priorities. Whether it's maximizing purchase price, minimizing closing costs, or securing favorable terms and conditions, defining your goals enables you to anchor your negotiation strategy and prioritize your bargaining positions. By identifying your non-negotiables and areas of flexibility, you can navigate the negotiation process with clarity and purpose.

Mastering negotiation requires effective communication and interpersonal skills. Successful negotiators listen actively, ask probing questions, and seek to understand the motivations and concerns of the other party. By building rapport, establishing trust, and demonstrating empathy, negotiators create an atmosphere of collaboration and goodwill, fostering constructive dialogue and paving the way for mutually beneficial outcomes.

Successful negotiators employ a variety of negotiation tactics and techniques to influence the outcome of negotiations. This may include framing the negotiation in terms of shared interests, exploring creative solutions to bridge differences, and using concessions strategically to build rapport and reciprocity. Additionally, understanding the concept of BATNA (Best Alternative to a Negotiated Agreement) empowers negotiators to assess their alternatives and leverage their bargaining power effectively.

In addition, successful negotiators conduct thorough research and preparation to bolster their negotiation position and anticipate potential objections or counteroffers. This may involve researching market conditions, comparable property sales, and local regulations to support valuation arguments, as well as identifying potential concessions or trade-offs to facilitate agreement. By coming to the negotiation table armed with information and insights, negotiators can enhance their credibility and persuasiveness, increasing the likelihood of a successful outcome.

Also, mastering negotiation requires the ability to remain calm, composed, and adaptable in the face of challenges or setbacks. Negotiations may encounter obstacles, conflicts, or impasses, requiring negotiators to remain flexible and resilient in pursuit of a resolution. By maintaining a positive attitude, reframing setbacks as opportunities for creative problem-solving, and focusing on long-term relationship building, negotiators can overcome obstacles and achieve successful outcomes.

In conclusion, "Mastering Negotiation: Closing Deals with Confidence" is a critical skill for real estate investors seeking to achieve success in the competitive and dynamic world of real estate investment. By defining clear objectives, communicating effectively, employing negotiation tactics and techniques, conducting thorough research and preparation, and maintaining composure and adaptability, investors can navigate the negotiation process with confidence and close deals that advance their investment objectives and maximize returns.

Renovation Strategies

"Transforming Properties into Gold: Renovation Strategies" is a transformative chapter that delves into the art and science of revitalizing properties to unlock their full potential and maximize investment returns. In this chapter, we explore the strategies, techniques, and best practices that empower investors to breathe new life into properties, enhancing their value, appeal, and profitability.

Renovation is more than just a cosmetic makeover; it's a strategic investment that can dramatically impact a property's desirability, functionality, and marketability. Whether it's updating outdated interiors, optimizing floor plans, or enhancing curb appeal, renovation strategies aim to align properties with market demands, attract quality tenants or buyers, and command premium rents or sale prices.

First and foremost, successful renovation strategies begin with a thorough assessment of the property's condition, market positioning, and investment potential. This involves conducting a comprehensive property inspection, identifying areas for improvement, and evaluating market trends, comparable sales, and rental rates to inform renovation decisions. By understanding the property's strengths, weaknesses, and market dynamics, investors can develop a renovation plan that maximizes ROI and enhances overall property value.

Effective renovation strategies prioritize upgrades that deliver the highest return on investment while aligning with target market preferences and demands. This may include focusing on high-impact improvements such as kitchen and bathroom renovations, flooring upgrades, or energy-efficient enhancements that enhance functionality, aesthetics, and livability. By investing strategically in renovations that resonate with tenants or buyers, investors can differentiate their properties in the market and command premium rents or sale prices.

Successful renovation strategies involve careful budgeting and project management to ensure renovations are completed on time and within budget. This may involve obtaining multiple bids from contractors, negotiating favorable pricing, and establishing clear timelines and milestones to track progress. Additionally, effective project management involves overseeing construction activities, addressing issues promptly, and maintaining open communication with contractors and stakeholders to ensure the successful execution of the renovation plan.

In addition, successful renovation strategies leverage technology and innovation to streamline processes, enhance efficiency, and optimize outcomes. Whether it's using virtual reality to visualize design concepts, adopting project management software to track progress, or implementing smart home technology to enhance property value, embracing innovation enables investors to stay ahead of the curve and deliver exceptional results.

Successful renovation strategies also involve a focus on sustainability and eco-friendliness to appeal to environmentally conscious tenants or buyers. This may include incorporating energy-efficient appliances, sustainable building materials, or water-saving fixtures that reduce utility costs and enhance the property's environmental footprint. By prioritizing sustainability in renovations, investors can attract a broader range of tenants or buyers and enhance long-term property value.

In conclusion, "Transforming Properties into Gold: Renovation Strategies" is a transformative guide that empowers investors to unlock the full potential of properties through strategic renovation. By conducting thorough assessments, prioritizing high-impact improvements, managing budgets and timelines effectively, leveraging technology and innovation, and embracing sustainability, investors can transform properties into lucrative investments that generate sustainable returns and enhance portfolio value.

Maximizing Income through Leasing

Maximizing Income through Leasing is a comprehensive guide that explores the strategies, tactics, and best practices for building and managing a profitable rental portfolio. In this chapter, we delve into the intricacies of leasing, offering insights and techniques to help investors optimize rental income, minimize vacancies, and maximize returns on investment.

Building a rental empire begins with acquiring properties that offer strong rental potential and align with your investment objectives. Whether it's residential, commercial, or multifamily properties, selecting assets in high-demand locations with favorable rental market conditions is crucial. Conducting thorough market research, analyzing rental rates, and evaluating property management potential are essential steps in identifying properties that can generate consistent rental income and long-term appreciation.

Once properties are acquired, effective leasing strategies play a critical role in maximizing rental income and occupancy rates. This involves implementing marketing initiatives to attract quality tenants, such as professional photography, online listings, and targeted advertising campaigns. Additionally, creating appealing rental listings that highlight property features, amenities, and location benefits can attract a larger pool of prospective tenants and command higher rental rates.

Successful leasing strategies involve setting competitive rental rates that balance market demand with the property's value proposition. Conducting comparative market analysis, monitoring local rental trends, and assessing property features and amenities enable investors to determine optimal rental pricing strategies. By striking the right balance between maximizing rental income and minimizing vacancy risk, investors can optimize returns and maintain a stable cash flow.

Effective tenant screening is a crucial component of successful leasing, ensuring that tenants are qualified, reliable, and compatible with the property's requirements. Conducting thorough background checks, verifying income and employment status, and obtaining references can help identify tenants who are likely to pay rent on time, maintain the property, and comply with lease terms. By selecting quality tenants, investors can minimize the risk of delinquencies, evictions, and property damage, thereby safeguarding rental income and property value.

In addition to tenant screening, proactive property management plays a pivotal role in maximizing income through leasing. This involves addressing maintenance issues promptly, providing responsive customer service, and fostering positive tenant relationships to encourage lease renewals and tenant retention. Additionally, implementing lease renewal incentives, such as rent discounts or upgrades, can incentivize tenants to extend their leases and reduce turnover costs.

Successful leasing strategies involve staying abreast of market trends and adapting to changing tenant preferences and demands. Whether it's offering flexible lease terms, incorporating amenities that appeal to modern renters, or embracing technology to streamline the leasing process, staying responsive to market dynamics enables investors to maintain a competitive edge and attract quality tenants in a competitive rental market.

In conclusion, "Rental Empire: Maximizing Income through Leasing" is a comprehensive guide that equips investors with the knowledge and strategies to build and manage a profitable rental portfolio. By selecting properties with strong rental potential, implementing effective leasing strategies, conducting thorough tenant screening, providing proactive property management, and staying responsive to market trends, investors can build a rental empire that generates consistent income, long-term appreciation, and lasting wealth.

Strategic Expansion

"Strategic Expansion: Scaling Your Portfolio Effectively" serves as a roadmap for real estate investors looking to grow their portfolios methodically and sustainably. In this chapter, we explore the strategies, considerations, and best practices for expanding your real estate portfolio with precision and foresight.

The journey of strategic expansion begins with a clear vision and defined objectives. Investors must articulate their long-term goals, whether it's achieving a certain level of passive income, building wealth for retirement, or leaving a legacy for future generations. By understanding your investment objectives, you can chart a course for strategic growth and align your expansion efforts with your overarching goals.

Strategic expansion involves conducting a comprehensive assessment of your current portfolio and resources. This includes evaluating the performance of existing properties, analyzing cash flow and returns on investment, and assessing your financial position and risk tolerance. By understanding your strengths, weaknesses, opportunities, and threats, you can identify areas for improvement and determine the optimal approach to portfolio expansion.

Successful strategic expansion requires a disciplined investment approach and a focus on diversification. This may involve diversifying across different asset classes, geographic regions, and investment strategies to spread risk and optimize returns. Additionally, adopting a balanced approach to expansion, considering factors such as market conditions, financing options, and exit strategies, enables investors to mitigate risk and capitalize on opportunities in varying market environments.

In addition, strategic expansion involves identifying and capitalizing on acquisition opportunities that align with your investment objectives and criteria. This may include targeting properties with strong income potential, favorable market conditions, and value-add opportunities that align with your investment strategy. By conducting thorough due diligence, negotiating favorable purchase terms, and structuring deals that optimize returns, investors can expand their portfolios with confidence and precision.

Successful strategic expansion requires a proactive approach to financing and capital management. This may involve exploring a variety of financing options, including traditional mortgages, private loans, equity partnerships, or creative financing techniques, to fund acquisitions and capitalize on investment opportunities. Additionally, optimizing capital structure and leveraging other people's money (OPM) enables investors to amplify purchasing power and accelerate portfolio growth while managing risk effectively.

Strategic expansion involves a focus on operational efficiency and scalability to manage a growing portfolio effectively. This may include implementing standardized processes and systems, leveraging technology and automation to streamline operations, and building a reliable network of property management and service providers to support portfolio growth. By investing in infrastructure and resources that facilitate scalability, investors can manage a larger portfolio efficiently and profitably.

In conclusion, "Strategic Expansion: Scaling Your Portfolio Effectively" is a guidebook for real estate investors seeking to grow their portfolios with precision and foresight. By defining clear objectives, conducting thorough assessments, adopting a disciplined investment approach, identifying acquisition opportunities, managing financing and capital effectively, and focusing on operational efficiency and scalability, investors can expand their portfolios strategically and achieve sustainable growth and success in the dynamic world of real estate investment.

Global Ventures: Exploring International Real Estate

"Global Ventures: Exploring International Real Estate" embarks on an exciting exploration of the vast opportunities and unique challenges presented by investing in international real estate markets. In this chapter, we delve into the intricacies of cross-border investment, offering insights, strategies, and considerations for investors looking to expand their horizons beyond domestic borders.

Investing in international real estate offers a world of possibilities, from diversifying portfolios and accessing new markets to capitalizing on emerging trends and tapping into global growth opportunities. However, venturing into international markets requires a nuanced understanding of cultural, regulatory, and market dynamics, as well as careful planning and due diligence to mitigate risks and maximize returns.

The first step in exploring international real estate is conducting thorough research and market analysis to identify promising investment destinations. This involves evaluating factors such as economic stability, political climate, legal framework, property rights, and currency exchange rates to assess the attractiveness and viability of international markets. By understanding the unique characteristics and risks of different countries and regions, investors can make informed decisions and identify opportunities that align with their investment objectives.

Successful international real estate investment requires establishing a strong network of local partners and advisors who can provide invaluable insights, expertise, and support on the ground. Whether it's collaborating with local real estate agents, legal professionals, or property managers, building relationships with trusted partners is essential for navigating foreign markets, overcoming language and cultural barriers, and ensuring smooth execution of investment transactions.

Exploring international real estate involves understanding the various investment structures and vehicles available for cross-border investment. This may include direct property ownership, real estate investment trusts (REITs), private equity funds, joint ventures, or crowdfunding platforms, each offering unique advantages and considerations. By evaluating investment options based on factors such as liquidity, transparency, tax implications, and diversification benefits, investors can select the most suitable vehicle that aligns with their investment strategy and risk profile.

In addition to selecting the right investment vehicle, successful international real estate investors pay careful attention to currency risk and foreign exchange considerations. Fluctuations in exchange rates can impact the value of investments and returns for foreign investors, highlighting the importance of hedging strategies and currency risk management techniques to mitigate exposure and preserve capital. By understanding the implications of currency movements and implementing appropriate risk mitigation measures, investors can safeguard their investments against adverse market conditions.

Exploring international real estate also involves navigating regulatory and legal complexities specific to each jurisdiction. This may include understanding local property laws, taxation rules, ownership restrictions, and licensing requirements, as well as compliance with anti-money laundering (AML) and know-your-customer (KYC) regulations. By seeking professional legal advice and conducting thorough due diligence, investors can ensure compliance with local regulations and mitigate legal and regulatory risks associated with cross-border investment.

Successful international real estate investors adopt a long-term perspective and embrace a diversified approach to portfolio allocation. Investing in international markets offers opportunities for diversification across geographic regions, asset classes, and currencies, reducing concentration risk and enhancing portfolio resilience. Additionally, maintaining a balanced portfolio that combines domestic and international investments enables investors to capitalize on global growth trends while mitigating country-specific risks.

In conclusion, "Global Ventures: Exploring International Real Estate" opens the door to a world of opportunities for real estate investors seeking to expand their horizons beyond domestic borders. By conducting thorough research, establishing local partnerships, understanding investment structures and vehicles, managing currency risk, navigating regulatory complexities, and adopting a diversified approach to portfolio allocation, investors can explore international real estate markets with confidence and unlock the potential for global growth and diversification.

Strength in Numbers: The Power of Real Estate Partnerships

"Strength in Numbers: The Power of Real Estate Partnerships" shines a spotlight on the collaborative potential that real estate partnerships offer for investors looking to amplify their success and expand their portfolios. In this chapter, we explore how strategic alliances, joint ventures, and syndication can leverage collective expertise, resources, and networks to unlock new opportunities and achieve mutual growth and prosperity.

Real estate partnerships harness the collective strengths of individual investors, pooling together capital, knowledge, and experience to pursue larger and more lucrative investment opportunities than would be possible alone. By joining forces with like-minded partners who share common goals and complementary skill sets, investors can mitigate risks, leverage synergies, and amplify returns on investment.

The power of real estate partnerships lies in the diversity of perspectives and resources that partners bring to the table. Whether it's financial resources, industry expertise, local market knowledge, or operational capabilities, each partner contributes unique assets and insights that enhance the overall strength and resilience of the partnership. By combining complementary strengths and leveraging shared resources, partners can achieve economies of scale, access new markets, and capitalize on opportunities that may be beyond the reach of individual investors.

Real estate partnerships enable investors to spread risk and diversify their portfolios across different asset classes, geographic regions, and investment strategies. By participating in joint ventures, syndications, or investment clubs, investors can access a broader range of investment opportunities and mitigate exposure to any single asset or market segment. Additionally, sharing risk among multiple partners can provide a buffer against market volatility, economic downturns, or unexpected events, enhancing overall portfolio resilience.

Real estate partnerships foster collaboration and learning opportunities among partners, enabling the exchange of knowledge, ideas, and best practices. By working closely with experienced partners, novice investors can gain valuable insights, mentorship, and guidance that accelerate their learning curve and increase their chances of success. Additionally, partnerships facilitate access to professional networks, industry connections, and deal flow, opening doors to new opportunities and expanding investors' reach within the real estate community.

In addition to financial benefits, real estate partnerships offer intangible advantages such as shared accountability, mutual support, and camaraderie among partners. By cultivating a culture of trust, transparency, and open communication, partners can navigate challenges, resolve conflicts, and celebrate successes together. Additionally, partnerships provide a platform for personal and professional growth, fostering collaboration, innovation, and continuous learning within the real estate community.

Real estate partnerships enable investors to leverage the expertise and resources of strategic partners to execute more complex or ambitious projects that may require specialized skills or capital-intensive investments. Whether it's acquiring large-scale commercial properties, developing multifamily housing complexes, or entering new markets, partnerships provide the flexibility and scalability to pursue diverse investment opportunities and achieve mutual objectives.

In conclusion, "Strength in Numbers: The Power of Real Estate Partnerships" underscores the transformative potential of collaborative ventures in the realm of real estate investment. By harnessing the collective strengths, resources, and expertise of partners, investors can amplify their success, mitigate risks, access new opportunities, and achieve mutual growth and prosperity. Whether it's forming joint ventures, syndications, or investment clubs, real estate partnerships offer a powerful mechanism for investors to leverage the strength of numbers and unlock the full potential of their investment endeavors.

Retire Rich: Real Estate as Your Key to Financial Freedom

"Retire Rich: Real Estate as Your Key to Financial Freedom" is a compelling manifesto that illuminates the path to financial independence and retirement security through strategic real estate investment. In this chapter, we embark on a journey toward building a prosperous future by leveraging the unique wealth-building potential of real estate.

For many, the dream of retiring rich may seem elusive, but real estate offers a proven pathway to turn this dream into reality. Unlike volatile stock markets or unpredictable investment vehicles, real estate provides tangible assets that generate predictable income, appreciate in value over time, and offer numerous tax advantages—all of which are instrumental in achieving long-term financial security.

At the heart of using real estate as a key to financial freedom lies the power of passive income. By acquiring income-generating properties—such as rental homes, apartment buildings, or commercial spaces—investors can establish reliable streams of cash flow that supplement or replace traditional sources of income. Unlike traditional employment, where income is tied to time and effort, passive income from real estate provides financial freedom by allowing investors to earn money while they sleep.

Real estate offers unparalleled opportunities for wealth creation through appreciation. Over time, properties tend to increase in value due to factors such as inflation, market demand, and economic growth. By leveraging the power of leverage—using borrowed capital to amplify returns—investors can accelerate wealth accumulation and multiply their equity through capital appreciation. This wealth-building potential is further enhanced by the ability to reinvest profits into additional properties, compounding wealth over time.

Real estate serves as a hedge against inflation and market volatility, providing stability and resilience in uncertain times. Unlike paper assets that can be eroded by inflation or wiped out by market downturns, real estate assets tend to preserve value and generate returns that outpace inflation over the long term. Additionally, real estate investments offer diversification benefits, helping investors reduce overall portfolio risk and navigate market fluctuations with confidence.

In addition to financial benefits, real estate investments offer numerous tax advantages that can significantly enhance returns and accelerate wealth accumulation. From tax deductions on mortgage interest, property taxes, and depreciation to capital gains tax exemptions on primary residences and 1031 exchanges for investment properties, the tax code offers a myriad of incentives for real estate investors to maximize profitability and minimize tax liabilities.

Real estate investments provide a tangible legacy for future generations, offering a means to pass on wealth and secure a lasting inheritance for loved ones. Unlike ephemeral assets that can be depleted or devalued over time, real estate assets endure as a tangible symbol of prosperity and security, providing a lasting legacy that transcends generations.

In conclusion, "Retire Rich: Real Estate as Your Key to Financial Freedom" is a beacon of hope and inspiration for aspiring retirees seeking a path to financial independence and security. By harnessing the wealth-building potential of real estate, investors can create a legacy of prosperity, achieve retirement goals, and enjoy the peace of mind that comes with financial freedom. Whether it's generating passive income, accumulating wealth through appreciation, enjoying tax advantages, or leaving a lasting legacy, real estate offers a powerful and proven pathway to retire rich and live life on your own terms.

Learning from Mistakes: Avoiding Common Pitfalls

"Learning from Mistakes: Avoiding Common Pitfalls" is a pivotal chapter that sheds light on the inevitable pitfalls and challenges encountered on the journey of real estate investment. In this chapter, we delve into the most common mistakes made by investors and offer invaluable insights and strategies to help navigate these pitfalls and achieve success in the dynamic world of real estate.

Real estate investment, like any other venture, comes with its share of risks and uncertainties. However, by learning from the mistakes of others and proactively mitigating potential pitfalls, investors can minimize losses, maximize returns, and build a resilient and profitable investment portfolio.

One of the most common mistakes made by novice investors is failing to conduct thorough due diligence before making investment decisions. Rushing into investments without adequately researching market conditions, property fundamentals, and potential risks can lead to costly mistakes and financial losses. By taking the time to analyze market trends, evaluate property fundamentals, and assess potential risks, investors can make informed decisions that align with their investment objectives and risk tolerance.

Also, another common pitfall is overleveraging or taking on too much debt without considering the potential consequences. While leverage can amplify returns in a rising market, it also magnifies losses in a downturn. Overleveraging can leave investors vulnerable to fluctuations in interest rates, rental income, or property values, increasing the risk of financial distress or foreclosure. By maintaining a conservative approach to leverage and ensuring that debt levels are sustainable, investors can mitigate risk and safeguard their financial stability.

Another common mistake is underestimating the importance of cash flow management and reserves. Insufficient cash reserves to cover operating expenses, vacancies, or unexpected repairs can leave investors vulnerable to financial setbacks and liquidity crises. By budgeting for contingencies, maintaining adequate cash reserves, and implementing proactive cash flow management strategies, investors can weather economic downturns and ensure the long-term viability of their investments.

In addition, another pitfall to avoid is neglecting to properly screen tenants or manage tenant relationships. Poor tenant selection or ineffective property management can lead to problems such as non-payment of rent, property damage, or legal disputes, resulting in financial losses and headaches for investors. By implementing rigorous tenant screening processes, maintaining open communication with tenants, and addressing issues promptly and professionally, investors can minimize tenant-related risks and maximize rental income.

Failing to adapt to changing market conditions or ignoring warning signs of market shifts is another common mistake. Real estate markets are inherently cyclical, with periods of expansion followed by contraction. Failing to recognize market trends or adjust investment strategies accordingly can result in missed opportunities or losses. By staying informed, monitoring market indicators, and remaining flexible in investment approach, investors can position themselves to capitalize on market opportunities and mitigate downside risks.

In conclusion, "Learning from Mistakes: Avoiding Common Pitfalls" serves as a guidebook for real estate investors seeking to navigate the challenges and uncertainties of the real estate market. By learning from the mistakes of others, conducting thorough due diligence, managing leverage and cash flow effectively, screening tenants rigorously, and staying vigilant to market trends, investors can minimize risks, maximize returns, and achieve long-term success in real estate investment.

Innovation in Action

"Innovation in Action: Tech Trends Transforming Real Estate" is a groundbreaking chapter that illuminates the transformative impact of technology on the real estate industry. In this chapter, we explore the cutting-edge technologies and trends reshaping the way we buy, sell, manage, and experience real estate, and how investors can harness these innovations to gain a competitive edge and unlock new opportunities.

Technology has revolutionized every aspect of the real estate lifecycle, from property search and transaction to construction and property management. By embracing the latest tech trends and innovations, investors can streamline processes, enhance efficiency, reduce costs, and deliver superior experiences for tenants, buyers, and stakeholders.

One of the most transformative tech trends in real estate is the rise of digital platforms and online marketplaces. From property listing websites and virtual tours to online auctions and crowdfunding platforms, digital platforms have democratized access to real estate investment opportunities and expanded the reach of investors beyond traditional boundaries. By leveraging digital platforms, investors can access a broader range of properties, conduct due diligence remotely, and transact seamlessly, eliminating geographical barriers and unlocking new markets.

Another game-changing tech trend is the advent of big data and analytics in real estate. By harnessing vast amounts of data from sources such as property listings, market reports, demographic trends, and social media, investors can gain valuable insights into market dynamics, identify emerging trends, and make data-driven investment decisions. Predictive analytics and machine learning algorithms enable investors to forecast market trends, assess risk, and optimize investment strategies with unprecedented accuracy and efficiency.

The emergence of smart buildings and Internet of Things (IoT) technology is another transformative tech trend. Smart building technologies, such as sensors, automation systems, and energy management platforms, enable real-time monitoring, optimization, and control of building operations, enhancing efficiency, reducing costs, and improving tenant satisfaction. By investing in smart building technologies, investors can create more sustainable, resilient, and technologically advanced properties that command higher rents and attract quality tenants.

In addition, another groundbreaking tech trend is the rise of blockchain technology in real estate. Blockchain, a decentralized and transparent ledger system, offers unprecedented security, efficiency, and transparency in real estate transactions. Smart contracts, powered by blockchain technology, enable automated and tamper-proof execution of real estate agreements, reducing transaction costs, minimizing fraud, and expediting the closing process. By embracing blockchain technology, investors can streamline property transactions, unlock liquidity, and create more transparent and efficient real estate markets.

Another transformative tech trend is the adoption of virtual reality (VR) and augmented reality (AR) technologies in real estate marketing and visualization. VR and AR enable immersive property tours, interactive floor plans, and virtual staging, allowing buyers and tenants to experience properties remotely and visualize spaces before making purchasing decisions. By leveraging VR and AR technologies, investors can enhance marketing efforts, attract more qualified leads, and accelerate the sales process, ultimately maximizing returns on investment.

In conclusion, "Innovation in Action: Tech Trends Transforming Real Estate" heralds a new era of opportunity and disruption in the real estate industry. By embracing cutting-edge technologies such as digital platforms, big data analytics, smart buildings, blockchain, and VR/AR, investors can revolutionize the way they invest, operate, and experience real estate. By staying ahead of the curve and harnessing the power of innovation, investors can gain a competitive edge, unlock new opportunities, and achieve sustainable growth and success in the dynamic world of real estate investment.

Generational Wealth with Real Estate

"Building a Lasting Legacy: Generational Wealth with Real Estate" is a visionary chapter that explores the enduring impact of real estate investment in creating and preserving generational wealth. In this chapter, we delve into the strategies, principles, and mindset required to build a legacy that transcends generations and leaves a lasting imprint on future heirs.

Real estate investment offers a unique opportunity to build a legacy that stands the test of time. Unlike other assets that may depreciate or diminish over generations, real estate has the potential to appreciate in value, generate passive income, and provide a tangible and enduring legacy for future generations.

One of the key principles of building a lasting legacy with real estate is taking a long-term perspective and adopting a generational mindset. Rather than focusing solely on short-term gains or immediate gratification, successful investors think strategically about how their investment decisions today will impact future generations. By taking a multi-generational approach to real estate investment, investors can create a legacy that benefits not only themselves but also their children, grandchildren, and beyond.

Building a lasting legacy with real estate involves instilling core values and principles of stewardship, responsibility, and financial literacy in future heirs. By educating children and grandchildren about the importance of real estate investment, teaching them financial management skills, and involving them in family investment decisions, investors can empower future generations to carry on the legacy and continue to grow and preserve wealth for years to come.

Diversification and risk management is another key principle of building a lasting legacy with real estate. While real estate can be a powerful wealth-building tool, it's important to avoid putting all your eggs in one basket. Diversifying across different asset classes, geographic regions, and investment strategies can help mitigate risk and safeguard against market fluctuations, economic downturns, or unforeseen events that may impact the value of real estate investments.

In addition, another essential element of building a lasting legacy with real estate is prudent estate planning and asset protection. By creating a comprehensive estate plan, including wills, trusts, and other legal instruments, investors can ensure that their real estate assets are transferred smoothly and efficiently to future generations while minimizing tax liabilities and preserving family harmony. Additionally, implementing asset protection strategies, such as asset titling, insurance, and entity structuring, can safeguard real estate assets from creditors, lawsuits, and other threats.

Also, building a lasting legacy with real estate involves a commitment to social responsibility and community engagement. By investing in properties that contribute positively to the community, such as affordable housing, sustainable development, or revitalization projects, investors can leave a legacy that extends beyond financial wealth and enriches the lives of future generations.

In conclusion, "Building a Lasting Legacy: Generational Wealth with Real Estate" is a testament to the enduring power of real estate investment in creating and preserving generational wealth. By adopting a long-term perspective, instilling core values in future heirs, diversifying and managing risk, implementing prudent estate planning and asset protection strategies, and embracing social responsibility, investors can build a legacy that transcends generations and leaves a lasting impact on the world.

Closing

In conclusion, "Get Rich: How to Build Long-Term Wealth Through Property Investment" serves as a comprehensive guidebook for aspiring real estate investors seeking to embark on a journey toward financial freedom and generational wealth. Throughout the pages of this book, we have explored the fundamental principles, strategies, and best practices for success in the dynamic world of real estate investment.

From laying the foundations of fortune through strategic property selection and investment planning to mastering the intricacies of negotiation, renovation, and leasing, each chapter has offered valuable insights and actionable advice to empower investors to navigate the complexities of real estate investment with confidence and foresight.

Moreover, we have examined the transformative power of technology and innovation in reshaping the real estate landscape, explored the benefits of collaboration and partnerships in amplifying success, and emphasized the importance of building a legacy that transcends generations through prudent estate planning, social responsibility, and community engagement.

As readers embark on their own real estate investment journey, it is essential to remember that success is not achieved overnight. It requires patience, perseverance, and a commitment to lifelong learning and continuous improvement. By embracing the principles and strategies outlined in this book, investors can unlock the full potential of real estate investment as a vehicle for building long-term wealth, achieving financial independence, and leaving a lasting legacy for future generations.

Ultimately, whether your goal is to retire rich, create a rental empire, or build a lasting legacy, the principles and strategies outlined in this book provide a roadmap to help you realize your aspirations and achieve success in the dynamic and rewarding world of real estate investment. May this book serve as a guiding light on your journey toward financial freedom, prosperity, and fulfillment.

www.ingramcontent.com/pod-product-compliance
Lightning Source LLC
Chambersburg PA
CBHW070347230526
45471CB00006B/2445